Copyright © 2021 Amesha Abigail Gray

All rights reserved

The characters and events portrayed in this book are fictitious. Any similarity to real persons, living or dead, is coincidental and not intended by the author.

No part of this book may be reproduced, or stored in a retrieval system, or transmitted in any form or by any means, electronic, mechanical, photocopying, recording, or otherwise, without express written permission of the publisher.

ISBN-13: 978-1-7780155-0-2

Cover design by: Mohhammad M. Rahman

Little Maurice's Visit to the HOSPITAL

The sun was at its brightest in a small Caribbean town called Faith. Little Maurice rolled over in bed to the sound of the rooster, only to find Mummy's spot next to him empty. He jumped out of bed to look for Mummy all over the house.

She was nowhere in sight! He thought.

It worried Little Maurice, so he starched his head in confusion. Just as he was about to hang his head low to cry, he remembered that he had not checked the kitchen yet. He ran to the kitchen in search of Mummy. There he saw her making breakfast for two.

"Good morning, Mummy. I woke up, and you were not beside me," he said sleepily.

"I got up early to make a special breakfast for you," Mummy said. Moments later, he took a shower in a Basin outside, got dressed and went to eat breakfast with Mummy under a mango tree.

After breakfast, he walked over to Nana's house, only 20 steps away. With his small fist, he knocked on the door and called out to Nana.

"Come in, Maurice…" Nana voice trailed off.

Opening the door quietly and slowly, he peeped inside and saw Nana eating a bowl of cornmeal porridge. Maurice sat beside her. Nana looked into his bright eyes and held her spoon in the air to offer some of her porridge.

He shook his head energetically from side to side to tell Nana, "No, thank you!" Suddenly, he was filled with excitement thinking about going to visit his best friend named Elijah. He tried to rush outside without distributing Nana, but Nana held on to his arm before he could leave.

"Trouble comes to those who find it, do not seek to find trouble, and it will not come to you, "she said in a preachy voice. "Always do what is right, and you will not find trouble," she explained. Maurice gave Nana a blank look, but nothing could ruin his day.

Feeling excited, he crossed the little bridge that separated his house from the other houses to get to the road. Where Maurice lives, the roadways are crowded with dirty, old, forgotten, and sometimes smelly trash.

But, in the eyes of a little boy like Maurice, it is trash, treasures, and toys. Once, he found items to make a toy truck: a body made from a carton box, wheels out of bottle caps, and axles out of long small sticks.

Although his carton box truck is homemade, it is the toy he cherished the most because he made it with Mummy.

He saw a big stick that fell from a tree on the side of the road. He picked it up, and that is when the idea came to him. His hand quivered, and his feet wobbled as he pretended to be a little old man.

"I am Grandpa," he mocked.

A few minutes later, Little Maurice reached Elijah's house. The front gate to the household was open without calling out to anyone in the home or knocking on the door, he raced inside to Elijah's room to play with his toys.

"Good morning Little Maurice," Ms. Hewlett greeted him.

Suddenly, the boys saw Mummy hurrying through the front gate with tears running down her cheeks.

"Why are you crying, Mummy?"

"I have bad news," she stooped down. She looked at the boys with grief.

Without explaining what had happened, she took Maurice into her arms. She walked to the road to take a taxi to go to a special place, the hospital.

He did not know what had happened, but he knew that hospitals are where sick people go to get better.

When they arrived at the hospital, they speedily ran to room 112, on the first floor. Maurice was surprised to see Nana fast asleep on the bed.

"It's too late Maurice, we missed Nana," Mummy explained. He felt clueless. He stared at Mummy, then glanced at Nana before he closed his eyes.

Little Maurice does not understand what his mother meant when she said, "it's too late." But he is happy to see Nana again.

He went over to the side of the bed and tried to wake her up. She did not answer, and he felt like Nana was ignoring him. His smile faded into a frown.

"Why is Nana ignoring me," he sniffled.

Mummy answered, "Nana is in a deep state of sleep because she is exhausted. Let her sleep. We can come to visit tomorrow," in the most comforting way

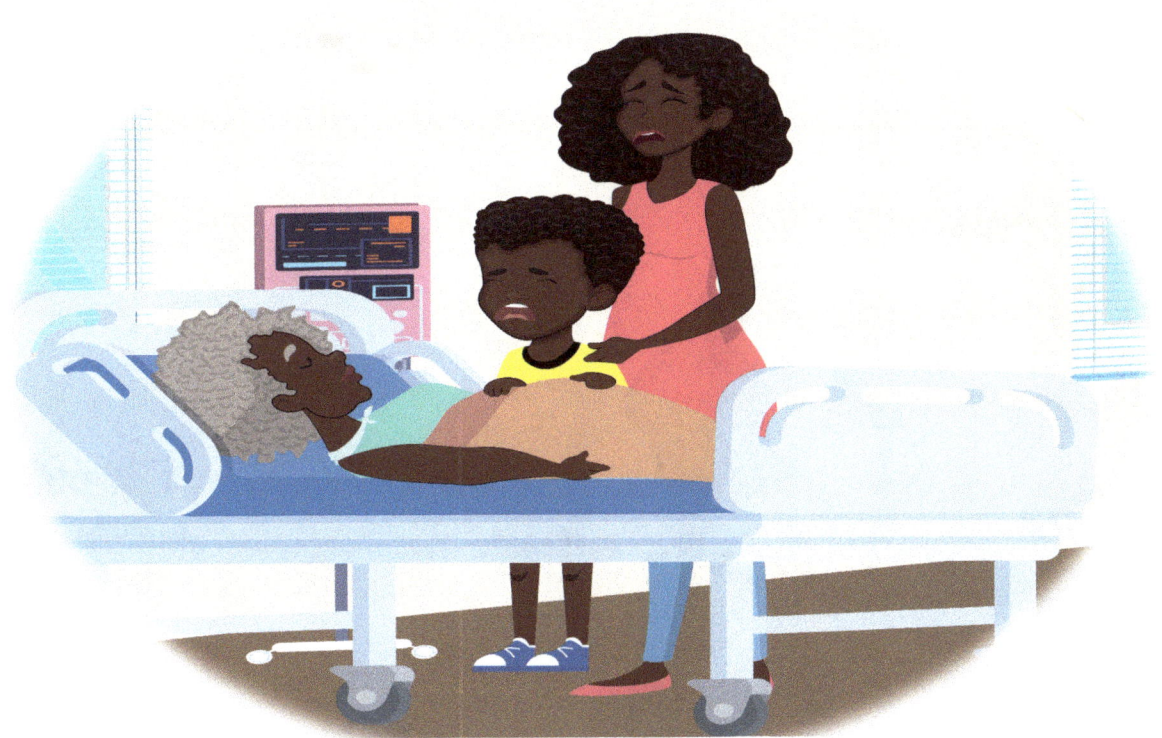

He screamed and cried, disregarding all the other patients, nurses, and doctors. He wanted Nana's attention.

"Nana went into a deep sleep. She will not be back home for a while. But do not worry, you will see her when she is out of the hospital."

"God does not love old people because they always go away," he says angrily.

"Yes, they do go away, but they always come back, just not when we need them to return home."

After he visited the hospital, life had changed for Maurice. Every morning, he woke up to the crow of the rooster and wondered if Nana would be awake or sleeping in her bed.

Each time he took a stroll to see her, he found an empty house where he sat on the front porch to sob. Maurice looked over yonder and continued to wonder. It was different for Mummy and him because he missed someone who meant a lot to him.

Wha' Gwan Fruits Puzzle

T	G	L	U	I	S	T	A	R	A	P	P	L	E
R	U	F	E	N	I	I	S	O	U	R	S	O	P
A	A	U	Y	M	F	N	S	I	L	R	L	P	A
S	V	A	S	R	U	I	I	P	J	P	E	T	S
I	A	N	F	U	L	L	I	G	A	T	R	E	S
P	S	G	U	I	N	E	P	G	I	U	S	T	I
L	T	F	I	E	O	A	T	E	B	A	U	R	O
S	A	L	S	A	G	K	S	R	N	U	T	E	N
E	R	O	U	E	P	S	U	E	U	U	J	R	F
F	F	S	O	R	F	A	A	P	B	A	J	F	R
L	R	N	R	M	A	R	J	A	F	E	S	I	U
P	U	J	A	C	K	F	R	U	I	T	R	U	I
T	I	P	A	C	A	R	A	S	F	J	A	R	T
L	T	A	J	U	L	I	E	M	A	N	G	O	Y

Passion Fruit

Jackfruit

June Plum

Naseberry

Star Apple

Guinep

Guava

Julie Mango

Star Fruit

www.ingramcontent.com/pod-product-compliance
Lightning Source LLC
Chambersburg PA
CBHW081205020426
42333CB00020B/2629